MW01703030

Workbook 2

SUPPLEMENT FOR

Power Tools
for the 21st Century

Can You live Off the Grid for 30 Days

By Dr. Richard Alan Miller

Workbook

2

SUPPLEMENT FOR

Power Tools

for the 21st Century

Can You Live off the Grid for 30 Days

Ram

By Dr. Richard Alan Miller

10-20-22

OAK

OAK Publishing

Organization for Advancement of Knowledge

OREGON, USA

Workbook 2

Exercise Supplement to Power Tools for the 21st Century

Can You live off the Grid for 30 Days

978-0-9883379-7-8

Copyright 2016 © OAK Publishing

All Rights Reserved

Published by

OAK Publishing

Grants Pass, OR 97527

541-476-5588

Cover & Interior Design

Elleyne Kase

No part of this material, including but not limited to, manuscripts, books, library data, and/or layout of electronic media, icons, et al, may be reproduced or transmitted in any form, by any means (photocopying, recording, or otherwise), without the prior written permission of Richard Alan Miller, the Publisher (and Author).

For general information on our other products and services please visit us at www.richardalamiller.com.

OAK

OAK Publishing

Organization for Advancement of Knowledge

Grants Pass, Oregon 97527 USA

PRINTED IN USA

Dedication

To Grace Thorn —a renaissance teacher, a close friend, and her work with children. She made this book "happen" for the City of Hollywood's co-sponsored Urban Survival Skills workshop (March 18-22, 2016) – with Mat Stein.

A special thanks to

Marie Zancanero, for help in putting the first Grid-less workshop together for Hawaii, 2011.

WIRED
The Non-Local
Holographic
MIND
POWER TOOLS
for 21st Century
Brain Drivers
Hemysync*
ESP & Hypnosis
Nono-technology
Virtual Audio
Eidetic Imaging
Legal Highs
Remap the Brain
XEROX®

Dr. Richard Alan Miller, Physicist
(1944-)

Richard Alan Miller is a pioneer in the annals of metaphysical and paranormal exploration. Miller began working in the "X-Files" world of Navy Intel (Seal Corp. and then MRU) in the late 60s. His public collaborations and research continue.

As an original black ops team-member, Miller's research in the field of paranormal began as a graduate physicist working 11 years with Navy Intel (Anesthesiology). During this period numerous foundational papers, including "A Holographic Concept of Reality" and "Embryonic Holography" were written.

His past and current writings and presentations reveal a depth of knowledge and practical experience in three major fields; Alternative Agriculture, New Age Physics, and Metaphysics.

Miller now writes for *Nexus* magazine and is a preferred guest on internet radio. He is re-emerging at a critical time in humanity's evolution where metaphysics and practical survival converge.

www.richardalanmiller.com and www.docram.com

Workbook 2 : EXERCISE SUPPLEMENT FOR
Power Tools for the 21st Century

Can You live off the Grid for 30 Days

Contents

"Things always work out

in the end.

If things are not working out,

it is not yet the end...."

— THOUGHT FOR THIS YEAR —

Introduction

To add fuel to the 2012 stigma, the official NASA website is now stating a new pending potential for disaster. They report a new set of solar flares within the next two years. While the normal solar storm cycle is every eleven years, this new set begins early next year. This new set of solar flares is predicted to be some of the largest ever recorded in history.

Mainstream scientific concern has grown since Issued by the National Academy of Sciences, it is titled "Severe Space Weather Events: Understanding Economic and Societal Impact." It details the potential devastation of the 2012 solar storms on our current planetary energy grid.

http://www.bing.com/videos/search?q=nasa+solar+flares+2012&qpvt=nasa+solar+flares+2012&FORM=VDRE

Because of the inter-linkages of our current The concern is a repetition of the 8-day 1859 "Carrington event," where a large solar flare accompanied by a coronal mass ejection (CME), flung billions of tons of solar plasma onto the earth's magnetosphere. This disrupted Victorian-era magnetometers and the world telegraph system.

The report outlines the worst case scenario for the US. The 'perfect storm' is most likely on a spring or autumn night in a year of heightened solar activity - something like 2012. Around the equinoxes, the orientation of the Earth's field to the sun makes us particularly vulnerable to a plasma strike. Sunspots are tangled knots of magnetism generated by the sun's inner dynamo.

A typical sunspot exists for just a few weeks. "Then it decays, leaving behind a 'corpse' of weak magnetic fields." The "conveyor belt" is a current phenomenon on the sun. It skims the surface of the sun, sweeping up the magnetic fields of old, dead sunspots. These magnetic knots (corpses) are dragged down at the poles to a depth of 200,000 km where the sun's magnetic dynamo can amplify them. Once the corpses are amplified, they become buoyant and float back to the surface, as new sunspots.

When (not if) this problem occurs, these flares will be like an ELF spike, where most devices using computer chips will cease to function – and, mostly need to be replaced. This would include telephones, your banking service, some automobiles, and certainly delivery systems (like food to local supermarkets). This disruption in our power grid will even extend to hospitals and basics (like those people with pacemakers).

The primary scientific concern is that the public is not prepared for these major inconveniences. Such situations like water from a well might need to be hand-pumped until power can be replaced. The report states that we should "expect delays in delivery systems" for up to two weeks at a time.

So, the BIG QUESTION is
"can you live off the energy grid for 30 days?"

A friend recalls when her daughter was five, they moved to a small cabin on a 240-acre woodlot. For the next five years they lived without electricity, phones, television, or computers, and used water from an above ground stream, which ran into a black plastic hosing. They chose to make this move so they would learn how to live well, if and when all other services failed.

Then, looking back, she recalls driving into town and calling her Mother. She was very upset because the electricity had gone out and she was unable to make breakfast. She remembered her daughter laughing out loud: "Are you going to be laughing and having a good time when all services stop?"

Or, are you going to join the masses in panic and fear? You have more resources than you know. Surviving a crisis safely requires an assessment of your means of survival NOW, when things appear fine.

With solar storms, the power grid alone may be down for up to two weeks. It may even require new parts (computer chips) before becoming functional again.

Chapter 1
Water

A person can live one month without food but only three days without water. For optimum health the amount of drinking water a person should consume is found by taking the weight of the person, dividing that by two, and drinking that number in ounces each day.

Someone who weighed 150 lbs. would need 75ozs. per day. There are 128 ounces in a gallon, so someone who weighs 150 lbs. needs to drink gallon a day. FEMA (Federal Emergency Management Agency), suggests, for emergencies, one should store at least one gallon of water per person per day.

However, individual water needs vary per person, depending on age, physical condition, activity and climate. Children, nursing mothers and ill people need more water. Plus, hot temperatures can double the amount of water needed.

The average person uses over 140 gallons of water each day for drinking, bathing, laundry, dishes and watering lawns. In a crisis situation water for bathing and washing clothes will be very hard to obtain, unless you live within walking (or biking) distance of a stream or lake. You may be able to carry washing water home, but there are some potential problems.

One gallon of water weighs 8.35 lbs - a five gallon bucket weighs over 40 lbs. Therefore, transporting water home may also be problematic. On level terrain a garden cart or a bike with baskets will work. If you must hand carry water over rough terrain, you will need a frame backpack rigged to carry gallons of water and it will need someone with a strong back to make it to the river and back.

First, the open water sources will most likely become polluted very quickly. For flushing a toilet this is not a problem. But, if you want to wash clothes or do dishes, contaminants in the water can still cause diseases and skin rashes. The Center for Disease Control receives over 4,000 cases each year of illness due to drinking contaminated water (dysentery, typhoid and hepatitis).

Every family should have in stock water purification tablets. Fifty (50) tablets cost about $4.99 and can be found on dozens of internet sites, at Wal-Mart, and most sporting good stores. Although this may make water safe to drink, it is advisable to also have a ceramic hand-operated water filter. Ceramic filters take 99.9% of all contaminates out of any water.

Hand-pump type filters cost anywhere from $30.00. Keep in mind the larger filters are more efficient, processing larger amounts of water. Boiling water for the recommended 10 minutes to kill organisms may not be an option, especially if fuel is not abundant. Boiling water will not remove chemical contaminants.

A toilet can be flushed with a bucket of water, but carrying it can quickly become tiresome. Most regular flush toilets use 1.98 gallons of water, while a low flush toilet 1.6. Toilets manufactured before 1994 use 4 gallons a flush. With a family of four, the possible water needs could be 10 to 24 gallons a day.

This means someone will need to carry between 85 to 200 lbs of water a day, just for the toilet. If you have pets, allow a minimum of one gallon per day for each dog or cat. This means for a family of four, 170 to 425 lbs of water per day is needed. This is 2 to 6 trips to the river (and back) each day.

In order to be prepared for this, you should take time to do a practice run and see how it works for you. Then, in a crisis, you will be prepared. For those who cannot reach or carry water at home, storage will be necessary. Collapsible containers, from Water Bob for $35, can be used in the bath tub to store approximately 100 gallons.

http://www.waterbob.com

At the very least you should have 7 gallons of pure water for each family member (enough for 7 days). It is time you to begin a survival plan, if you should need to "go off the grid for 30 days." For basic survival equipment for water, begin at

http://www.equipped.com/toc.htm

Basic Survival Equipment

http://www.equipped.com/toc.htm

http://www.baproducts.com/index.asp

http://www.survivalcenter.com/scallion.html

food

Chapter 2

Food

When you ask the typical American what he will do in a food shortage crisis, a common response is: "I will get a gun and kill my own game". Even in parts of the nation where game is plentiful, the most seasoned hunters don't get game every year. Hunting should be considered a very bad option, especially in the more urban areas, like New York City.

So what are some of the options for food in a "Grid-Less" crisis? These include: saved food, produced food, stolen or poached food, and wild crafted food. Clearly, storing some food for a crisis is your best option. The question then becomes what to store. Before you buy bags of soybeans, consider some of the American diet facts.

Americans eat a whopping 3,000 to 4,000 calories a day. 25 – 30% of those calories are sugar. If you drink sodas, sweet coffees, power drinks, and eat sweet "low fat foods," you may be getting 25 % of your calories in sugar alone. A 2-liter Pepsi has 224 grams of sugar, just shy of 1/2 lb. (53 teaspoons).

Recently, the U.S. D. A. researched the top nine sources of calories in the average American diet. In a time of crisis you will not feel well or be able to focus and function if you attempt to change from this "American diet" to "soy beans and rice". Here is that list:

Whole Milk

Cola

White Bread

Rolls

Sugar

2% Milk

Ground Beef

White (Wheat) Flour

Processed American Cheese.

To "get by," most people need 1,500 calories and 75 grams of protein, each day.

At 1500 calories per day, one loses weight and will feel hungry, however, it is enough food to sustain a person. If water and fuel are scarce, canned foods may be one's best option. Pre-cooked canned foods contain water, and can be eaten cold.

Try this one day test diet and see how you get by. Purchase one 15-oz. can of chili with beans (580 calories), one 5-oz. can of tuna (100 calories), one can green beans (50 calories), one 29-oz. can of sliced peaches (600 calories), and one pack of Top Ramen – 3-oz. (380 calories). Total calories = 1,710. Grams of protein =76, and grams of sugar =131 grams. The cost = $5.00, for only one day.

Using this model you will have to buy and store 120 cans of food and 30 packs of noodles for each person in your household for 30 days.

If you have a large coffee (or other addiction), be sure to buy extra amounts of those items. The advantage of canned food is low cost, and the storage time is reasonable (two years).

If water is plentiful, you may want freeze dried foods for your stash. There are numerous sources on the internet to buy freeze dried food products. You can purchase a 7-day 2-person pack for $110.69 ($7.80 per person per day). Freeze dried foods have a very long shelf-life, take up very little space, and offer, a very good variety.

http://survivalacres.com/

If you have limited money, buy

15 lbs of pinto beans

4 lbs. of lard

25 lbs. of rice

5 lbs. of sugar

box of salt

These foods will store well and only cost $2.50 per day per person.

The wild crafting option is also possible if you live in or near a green belt. When wild crafting for food, remember: the more landscaped the setting, the more likely it is to be toxic. Almost all organic gardens and landscapes are wild and tangled. Most manicured landscapes are maintained with fungicides and herbicides and very toxic to eat.

If you imagine yourself wild-crafting, buy books on wild edibles and study them ahead of time. Don't taste plants to see if they are edible. There are just too many poisonous plants for this to be a safe option. A simple test, that is almost always correct, is to scratch your skin on the inner arm. Then rub the plant into the skin. If it puckers or becomes irritated, most likely it is toxic (or allergenic)

The production of food is a good option in a crisis, but will take some planning. Fresh sprouts are tasty and very easy to grow. You can produce sprouts by spreading seeds on a towel that has been spread out on a cookie sheet. If kept damp, the sprouts will be ready to eat within 6 days.

Seeds, such as sunflower, broccoli, radish, alfalfa, and clover sprout well. You can buy seed singles or sprouting mixes from Johnny's Select Seeds (Maine) or Richters Herbs (Canada). Both carry 1 oz. bags of sprout seeds, at good prices ($3.50 each).

http://www.Johnnyseeds.com

http://www.richters.com

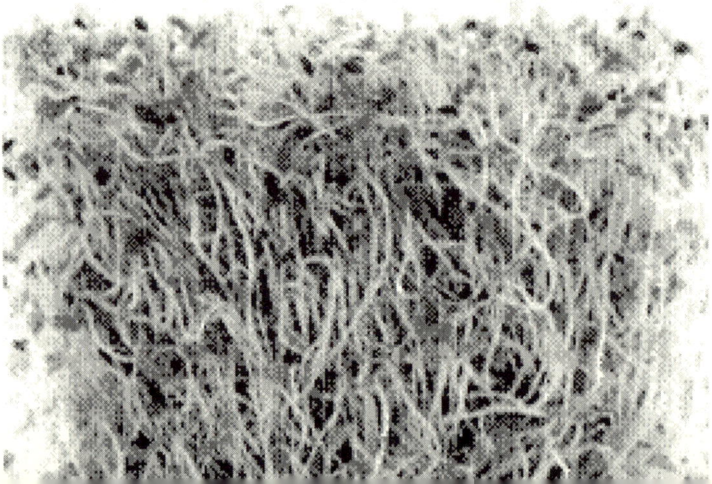

Another way to store food is by smoking it. If you have one or more freezers of meat, and the power goes out, all that food will begin to thaw and spoil. With a smoker, you can make good use of your meat that would otherwise spoil. A smoking project will keep you occupied in the first days, when you need to stay busy.

The bottom line is you need to plan ahead. It is most certain that we are going to experience food shortages in the next several years. If you are prepared and have a plan, you and your family can come through the experience with a sense of adventure and success, rather than fear and panic.

basic medical needs

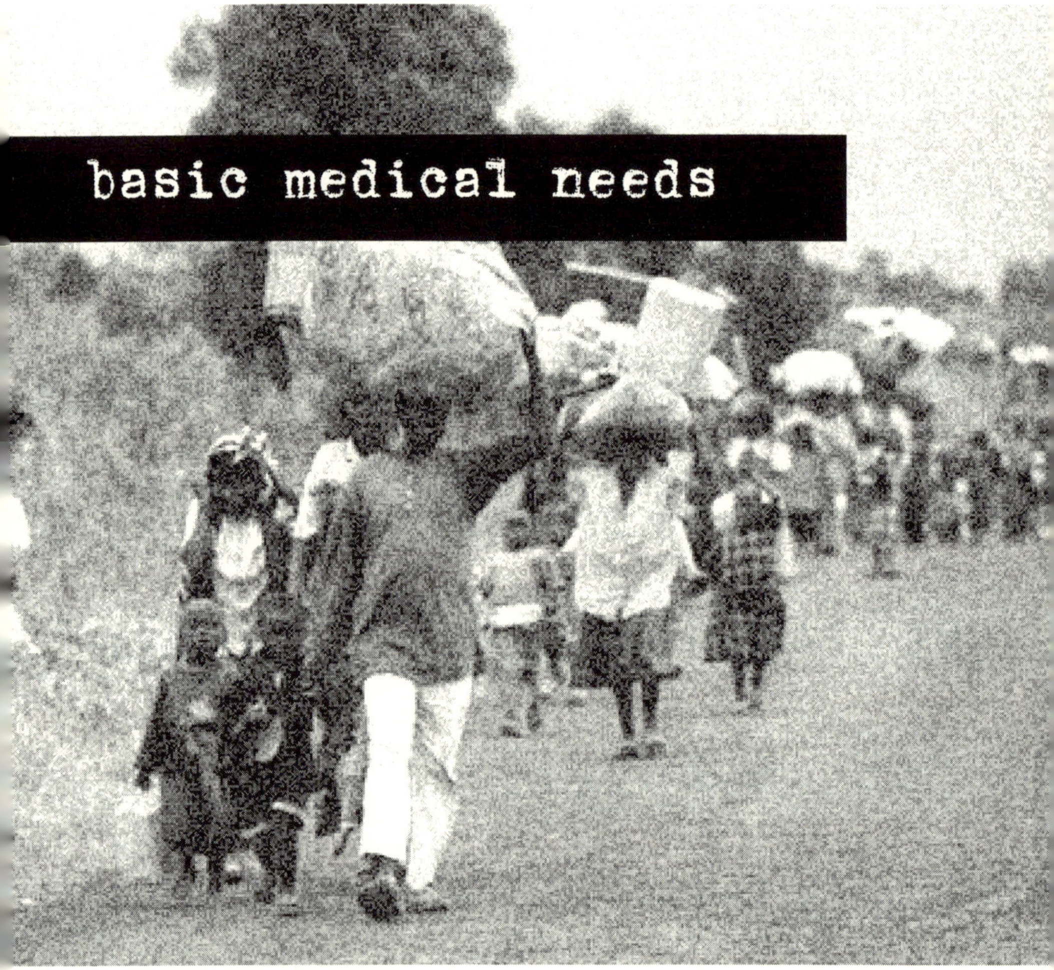

Chapter 3

Medicine

In every disaster or disruption of services, there are illnesses and deaths that cannot be avoided. There are also illnesses and deaths that can be avoided. Historically, it doesn't matter if the disaster is an earthquake, flood, or tornado, the basic medical needs and problems remain very similar.

The main causes of illnesses and death are

dehydration,

physical exhaustion,

heat exhaustion,

food poisoning,

failure to take prescribed medication,

accidents after the trigger event, and

secondary diseases from poor sanitation.

Anyone who has a prescription drug that must be taken every day should always have a one to three months supply on hand. Ideally, the medication should be kept in a small travel bag.

If and when you do leave the house, you should always carry medication with you. You may not be able to come back, due to unforeseen events. Also, one of the first items stolen during break-ins are prescription drugs. It could take weeks or months for the supply of your medication to become available again.

Dehydration is a huge problem in the aftermath of most disasters. If you feel thirsty you are already 2% dehydrated. Like an automobile engine, you are a quart low on water. When total fluid-loss reaches 5%, your body will become damaged (much like your car), and you begin to die.

When the body reaches 10% fluid loss,
emergency help is needed IMMEDIATELY.

Most 10% fluid loss (or above) is often fatal! These are the following effects of dehydration normally experienced:

increased heart rate

increased respiration

decreased sweating

decreased urination

increased body temperature

extreme fatigue

muscle cramps

headaches

nausea

tingling of the limbs

Making sure you drink enough fluids is very important. There are a number of illnesses that add to and/or cause dehydration. These include flu, vomiting, diarrhea etc. Any illness that causes fluid loss should be immediately treated. If you have zero access to any liquids, you can save your life by drinking your own urine. Recalling the movie *Dune*, urine is a sterile, salty liquid that will keep you alive.

Food poisoning is another common problem during a disaster situation. Everyone hates to throw out food, but the food in your fridge will only be safe to eat if it remains cold. Usually, this is less than 24 hours after the power goes off. To keep food from spoiling, it must be kept hot at 140 degrees F. (in a pan, on a wood stove), or kept cold.

Food (in a container) can be put on an outside deck or porch when it is cold outside (less than 40 degrees F.). If you have a very cold running stream, you can keep your food in a bucket in the stream. Otherwise, do NOT eat food that has been sitting at room temperature for more than one day.

There is a science to basic food preservation and what foods need for safe temperature storage. For when to chill or not to chill, go to

http://busycooks.about.com/library/lessons/blrefrig.htm

Activated charcoal is very important to have on hand. It will stop vomiting and diarrhea, and will absorb toxins, including bacteria and germs. Slippery elm tea is sometimes the only thing that can stop vomiting, and help someone to hold down liquid. The powder is made into a tea and fed by the spoonful, until the person can drink a cup or more.

Exhaustion can occur when a person feels they are overwhelmed, and the situation seems hopeless. Exhaustion can also cause other serious latent problems such as a heart condition, high blood pressure, and suicidal tendencies. Staying calm and pacing yourself is very important. A useful sleep aid is the mint-herb Skullcap, a mildly sedating pain-killer (helps calm agitation).

You must avoid becoming overheated, wet, or chilled. Drinking alcohol of any kind adds to dehydration and makes one less resistant to cold. Meanwhile, not drinking enough water will make a person more prone to heat exhaustion.

Because all resources for sanitation may be scarce, it is very important to have the following items in your survival kits:

hand sanitizer (or a hand soap)

disposable gloves

rolls of gauze (several sizes)

tweezers

scissors

flashlight (with spare batteries)

sterile wipes

water proof band-aids (several sizes)

Often called a *Go Bag*, this might be where your prescription drugs are carried. The Go Bag should also hold a first aid kit that is more extensive than something from a bathroom. A tactical field trauma kit might be more useful than just band-aids. In a crisis, you are more liable to encounter serious injuries than simple cuts and bruises.

http://www.adventuremedicalkits.com/

There are many other items that can help preserve your well being. Some are foods, but considered as medicines. Packets of electrolytes (like Emergen-C), can be added to water to prevent heat exhaustion. Grapefruit seed tablets are a natural first line of defense when feeling ill.

composting_toilet

Chapter 4

Sanitation

Our sanitation in the United States is based on water. We use gallons of hot, steaming and soapy water. If the grid goes down and the water stops flowing, most of America will be unprepared for a household sanitation system that does not involve water. It is, however, critical that we get ready for that possibility and know what to do.

Simply knowing how to clean and sanitize your hands can save your life or the life of your child. Washing one's hands with soap, for example, could slash diarrhea cases by nearly 50%, and "save at least 1 million lives per year" (World Bank). 50% of all deaths in children under the age of 5 are due to diarrhea, caused by poor sanitation.

Over 15 funguses, bacteria, and viruses are commonly found under long fingernails, including *Staphylococcus*. One of the first actions to take for good sanitation when the grid goes off line is to cut your fingernails as short as possible. If very little water is available, every family should have hand sanitizers in their emergency supplies and use them often.

A high percent of contamination is hand to mouth, so wash or sanitize your hands every time you touch a pet, gather materials in the woods, or use the bathroom. Always sanitize your hands before preparing food or gathering water. Have a good supply of disposable gloves for "messy jobs," especially when changing diapers.

In our present world, UNICEF says you will find approximately 10 million viruses, 1 million bacteria, 1,000 parasite cysts, and 100 parasite eggs - just in one gram of human excrement.

If you live in a single family home and you have water nearby, you will most likely be able to flush your toilet. But, if the plumbing stops working, you should know how to make a 5 gallon bucket composting toilet. My friend had one in a cabin in the woods for years, and had no problems.

You will need 2 heavy duty 5-gallon buckets, a 5-lb pound bag of garden lime, compost, and a toilet seat. The compost can be dry grass clippings, leaves, sawdust, small wood chips, or peat moss. If there isn't very much plant material in your area, you can buy a cube of peat moss. It works well, and will last a long time.

Take your bucket and put about 4 inches of peat moss in the bottom. Place the toilet seat on it and you are ready to go. When the "deed" is done, sprinkle a tablespoon of lime, and cover with an inch of peat moss (or leaf debris). Keep using this bucket until it is full or begins to smell. When that happens, place the bucket outdoors, to air and dry out, and then switch to the other bucket.

When the second bucket is full, empty the first into a 55-gallon drum for holding, or into a pit in the ground. Keep in mind that it is not legal to dump waste onto the ground, and should NEVER be dumped into any water system. For more info on the bucket toilet go to:

http://www.omick.net/composting_toilets/bucket_barrel_toilet.htm

bleach is your friend

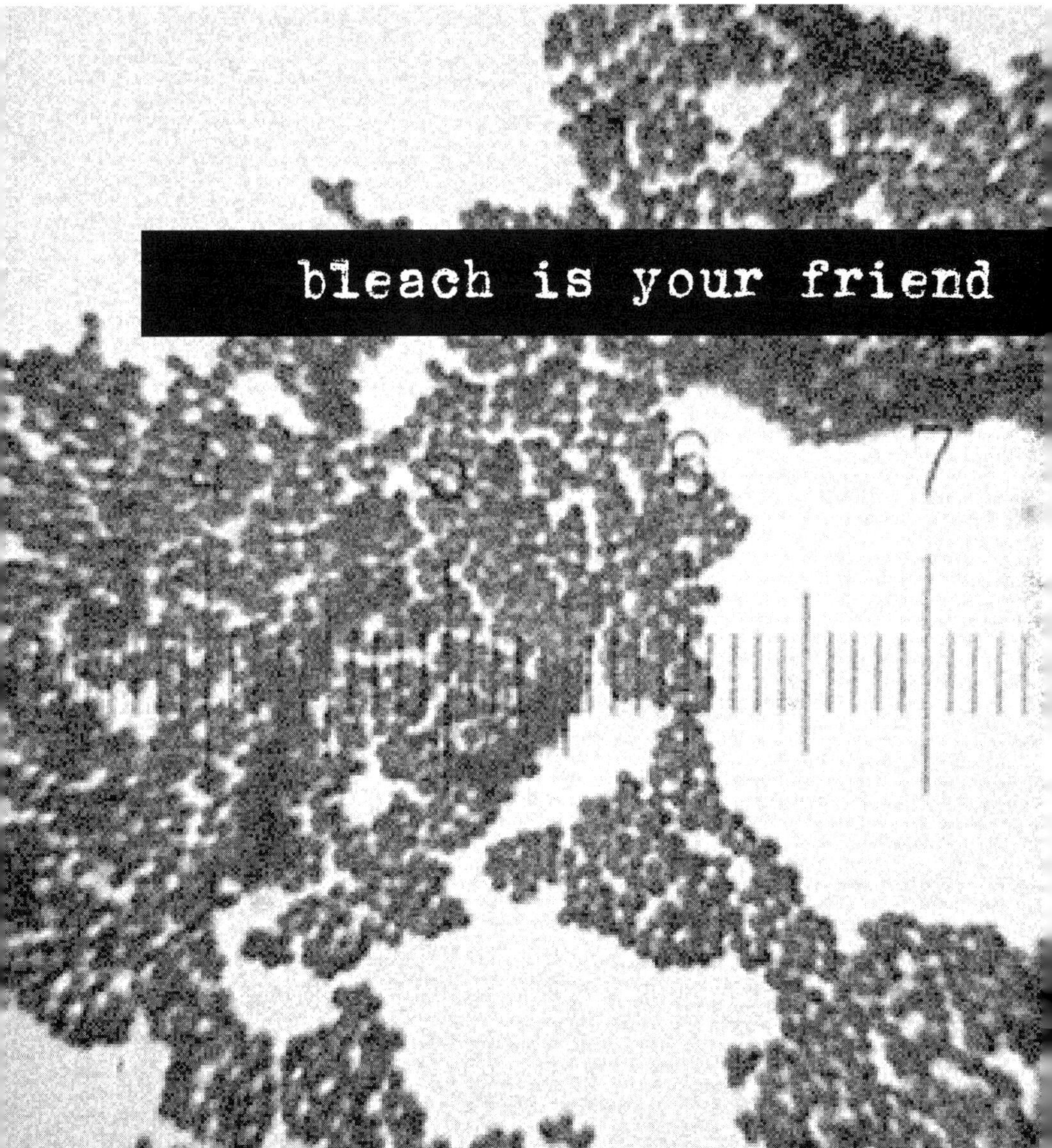

When it comes to sanitation, bleach is your friend.

3/4 cup of regular, unscented household bleach added to 1 gallon of water can be used to wipe down and disinfect surfaces. Bleach and water will kill such pests as *Salmonella, Pseudomonas, Streptococcus, Escherichia coli* (aka *E. coli), Shigella dysenteriae, Staphylococcus aureus* (MRSA), and even *Candida albicans* (yeast).

Dishes, pots, pans, and other cooking utensils can be rinsed in bleach water to prevent spreading pathogens. You can avoid dish-washing by lining bowls and plates with wax paper, and then using the dirty paper as a fire starters.

If you have to wash your clothes in a questionable source of water, rinse your clothes in bleach water to avoid staph (or other infection) on your skin. At the very least, rinse your underwear in bleach water, and then dry them in the sun. Sunshine is a good disinfectant on most items. All dirty underwear has parasite eggs in them. These can become air born, and spread from person to person, causing diarrhea.

If you do not have a water filter, you can make dirty water drinkable by filtering it through a cloth to take out big particles. Then, add 4 drops of bleach to each quart of water. Pouring it from one container to another for several minutes will make it drinkable.

The bottom line in sanitation is to see everything as contaminated. One must be very careful not to spread germs from one source to another and to your family. Practicing awareness of extreme sanitation ahead of time will help you keep your family healthy during a crisis.

fuel

ALCO BRITE
COOK'n'HEAT
FUEL
INDOOR
OUTDOOR
COOK FOOD · BOIL WATER · KEEP WARM

Chapter 5

Heat & Fuel

Keeping warm (or cool) without gas or electricity requires absolute planning. In the 12th hour after the grid goes down, you may not be able to gather enough fuel to keep warm.

If your home has a working fire place or wood stove, now is the time to acquire wood. Depending on how cold it gets, a family that heats with wood can use two to five cords in winter, or about one cord a month. If you plan to use wood heat as a backup, you should have at least one cord of dry wood under cover or under a tarp.

You can maximize your heat output with a "Grate Wall of Fire," an efficient fire burning design. When you are using wood, you want the greatest amount of heat possible projecting into the room. Some people bring a cold draft in from outside, using a small 2-inch hose from under the house. This draft makes the fire burn hotter.

Without wood as a backup, you will need another heat source. One of the best options is alcohol. Alcohol burns very hot and clean. It is safe to use indoors, unlike other fuels (such as wood) that need to be vented. In Brazil, many families heat their rooms by pouring a small amount of rubbing alcohol in a heavy-duty frying pan, placed on a brick and lit with a match.

A safe form of alcohol for heat is gel alcohol. Normally sold in a small can (like Cook 'n Heat), gel-alcohol has a 4 to 5 hour burn time, (depending on altitude and oxygen supply). It can produce up to 2,500 BTU's of heat per hour.

When boiled with weak sulfuric acid, potato starch is changed into glucose, and this can then be fermented into alcohol. You can then make gel-alcohol from left-over bi-products, and this does not require an expensive stove or facility. Gel-alcohol is simple to make, using bi-products (egg shells, vinegar, and water).

http://zenstoves.net/Sterno.htm

As a last resort, burning 150-proof rum may be better than drinking it. Preparing old and rotting fruit (or vegetables) into mash to produce alcohol is easy. Yeast speeds up this process, as glucose sugars break down into alcohol.

www.homedistiller.org/wash-fruit.htm

Heat can be maximized by keeping your body warm and dry. You should dress in layers, but not allow the body to perspire. Perspiring is for cooling the body, and can actually cause hypothermia. As a survival tool, all forms of wool (including alpaca) heat when they become wet and will always keep your body warm and dry.

Most heat loss is also from the top of the head, so always wear a hat. Again, wool is best. Sitting or standing on a cold surface will cause body heat loss through transference, so make sure a blanket or other form of insulation is placed between all cold surfaces and your warm body.

In extreme cold, try to heat only one primary room of your home, not the whole building. If there is a basement, the temperature will be more moderate there, and it will hold the heat better. Use duck tape, towels, blankets, or even newspaper to cover windows to prevent heat loss.

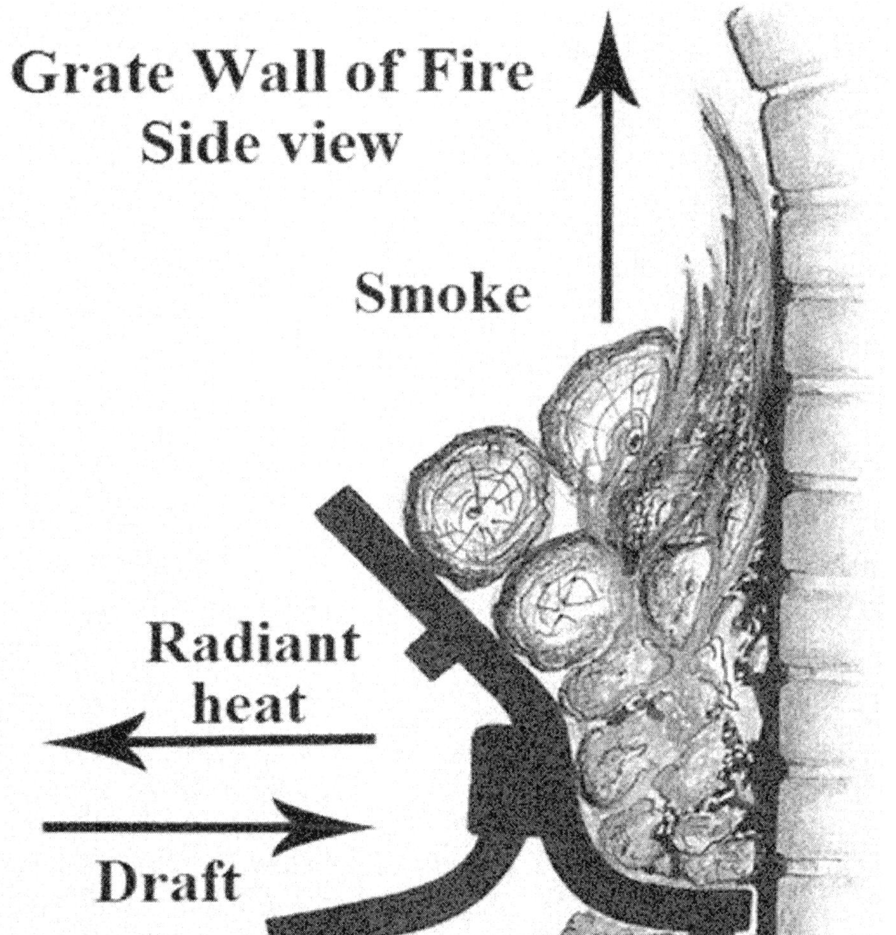
Grate Wall of Fire
Side view
Smoke
Radiant
heat
Draft

Drinking plenty of water helps to keep you warm. When a person becomes dehydrated, the body cannot maintain heat as well. You can also warm your body with specific herbs. Ginger in hot tea will warm you longer than black tea alone. Also chili pepper, garlic, black pepper, cardamom, and cinnamon will help elevate body temperatures.

A great way to cook without fuel is solar. Even on a low-light day, you can cook your food or pasteurize water for drinking using the sun. If you want to make a solar cooker, the process is simple and there are numerous ways to go. You will only need aluminum foil, cardboard, and glue.

http://solarcooking.org/plans/funnel.htm

Food can be kept cool with the *Pot-in-Pot Cooling System.* This is a simple-to-implement evaporative cooler, consisting of one pot inside another. Wet river sand in between each pot, and a damp cloth is placed on the top. When kept in a dry, well-ventilated and shady location, water evaporates and cools the inner container.

With this simple technology, eggplant can last 27 days rather than three. Spinach can be kept for 12 days, instead of spoiling after one day. Tomatoes and peppers stay fresh for three weeks.

http://www.ehow.com/how_7610692_make-potinpot-preservation-cooling-system.html

The best way to keep a house or apartment cool is to keep the heat out. Most heat comes in through the windows, especially when the sun shines on them. Your windows work like a solar cooker, heating up the inside of the building. To keep the building cool, open all windows at night to let all hot air flow out.

In the morning, close all windows to trap the cold air inside. If you live in an area that has very hot temperatures, cover windows with cardboard that has aluminum foil glued to on one side. These reflective covers will make a big difference and can be done ahead of time and stored in the garage.

This same concept can be carried a step further with the roof of the home. A tarp can be painted with reflective paint and put on the roof during the hot season. Anyone that has ever been on a roof in the summer knows how very hot the roof gets. A tarp on the roof may not be beautiful, but it will keep the house cooler.

entertainment

Chapter 6

Entertainment

When man is at his wit's end, is also when he shows his diversity in both wit and humor.

Five days after the tsunami hit Japan, the government told people to stay indoors. The power is out, food is scarce, fuel is low, and it is extremely cold. So imagine that you are now stuck inside for an extended period of time. What are you going to do?

When we lose something or someone dear, we go through a grieving process. Many people in today's society love their cyber-toys (blackberry, computer, cell phone, iPod and Xbox). In other words we love "the Grid," and will grieve when it is lost. There are five stages of grief: Knowing these steps offers direction and recourse.

From *The Book of Enoch*, it is said: "Once you have the demon's name, you now also have control of the demon."

Denial - At first you will tend to deny the grid has gone down. You may even knock on your neighbor's door and ask "Is this really happening?"

Anger- You will then become furious at the world for letting your beloved "Grid" go down. You may even throw your blackberry across the room, in frustration....

Bargaining - Now you make bargains with God, asking, "If I do this, will you bring back my internet?"

Depression – When God does not seem to care, you then feel numb. Sadly, you sit and stare at your pile of electronics, feeling sad and depressed.

Acceptance - Your anger, sadness and mourning will eventually taper off. Desperate for entertainment you begin to face the loss and look for something to do.

In less time than you can imagine, boredom begins. People will do anything to avoid boredom. Entertainment will have to come in other forms.

Entertainment consists of any activity which provides a diversion, or permits people to amuse themselves in their leisure time.

The ancient practices of storytelling can have real value and entertainment when everyone is stressed and needs something else to think about (diversion). "The never-ending story" is when one person starts a story, and (at some point), hands it over to the next person to add something more.

"*Near the sea, a small foot-path winds to the top of...*" Then, the next person adds a line, and a story begins to unfold. With practice, this can become very entertaining, and you might be surprised who in your family (or circle of friends) has been holding back their story-telling ability.

Other oral traditions include poetry and ballads. What if you decided to only speak in rhyme for an entire day? Or once each day, everyone had to present their best poem for the day. These could become a way of looking back at what you went through at the time and how you and your family got through it. This is the art of story-making and how urban myths are created.

GO
GO

Boredom comes from the inability to focus the mind. Two time honored ways to overcome your lack of focus are through Yoga and meditation. Richard Hittleman's book *Yoga: 28 Day Exercise Plan* is an excellent program that will take anyone from zero to success in twenty eight days. These gentle exercises will calm the nerves, and relax the body.

Another reason people become bored is that they are not using their minds. Strategy and board games (like cards, Chess, or Go) help focus the mind, and helps to relieve boredom. Music, singing and dancing always lifts the spirit, and using unusual ways of expression (like spoons) inspires comedy.

Making crafts and art is another good diversion, especially when you do it around survival needs (like candle making). *Origami*, the art of folding paper, was used in the movie Blade Runner. Anything that takes concentration and repetitive skills will help sharpen the brain and relieve boredom. It has been said that an active brain is never bored.

Being creative is one of the oldest ways of entertaining. As hordes of zombies try to eat you, you should give your aspect of creativity more serious thought. Keeping a diary or some kind of journal is a great way to keep occupied and sane (like *"The Diary of Ann Frank"*). Often called your "magical memory," a daily diary is a snap-shot of each moment.

Chapter 7
The Go Bag

You have just learned that a major disaster is about to happen to your home, and you have 15 minutes to prepare what you need and leave for safer shelter. You can only take what you can carry, and may never be allowed to return for things forgotten. What exactly should you take, and why?

A *Go Bag* is basically a big survival kit that contains all of the items you would require to survive after a disaster. A *Go Bag* allows you to grab what you need quickly and evacuate should a disaster happen.

Most experts suggest that your *Go Bag* should contain enough supplies to last at least 72 hours (3 days). Since most major disasters can disrupt services and normal life for longer periods, we think it is a good idea to have a Go Bag that will allow you survive for an indefinite period of time.

Make sure your *Go Bag* is built to fit your needs. Some people may need items that are not listed. Remember that this is a guideline, meant to help you get your bag together. When putting your bag together, remember to take into consideration any special needs or items that you or your family might need (medications).

If you have a large family, you may want a special *Go Bag* for each child. Make sure it is light enough for them to carry. Getting your family involved in being prepared can be a life-saver if something happens where one or both parents are not present at the time of the event.

Your *Go Bag* should not weigh more than 20 lbs for adults and about 5 lbs for small children. Make sure it is comfortable to carry. Once you get your *Go Bag* together, take a hike for at least one hour and see how you feel. It is possible you may have to walk for several days, and it would be best if you were prepared for that possibility.

In Japan the government was telling people to get 50 miles away from certain areas. With a family carrying supplies and traveling through a disaster area, 50 miles could be a 3- or 4-day walk.

The *Go Bag* Contents Check-List:

A Disaster Plan - Includes location of emergency areas, rallying points, multiple evacuation routes, maps of the area, trail maps, etc. Maps that show the local rail routes can be very useful because they are often the most direct route to follow from one town to another. (Use a water proof laminate to protect the plans).

First Aid Kit - Have together large band aids and antiseptic cream. Learn to make a butterfly band aid out of tape (even duck tape). A good butterfly band aid will work better than stitches

Survival Manuel - This should be studied before hand and kept for reference during a disaster. We use the *SAS Survival Handbook: How to Survive in the Wild, in Any Climate, on Land or at Sea When All Hell Breaks Loose* - US Army Survival Manual: FM 21-76

Clothing - Socks, gloves, rain suit, poncho, jacket, hat, bandanas, and clothing for your environment

the go bag

Assorted Knives, and a small stone to sharpen them.

Camp Axe & Camp Shovel

Flashlights – Recommend solar or the type that wind up or shake.

Radio – A portable CB or Ham Radio that winds up, rather than one that uses batteries.

Fire Starter – A flint is best, or water-proof matches, found at most Army-Navy stores.

Multi-Tool – Swiss Army knife, with everything on it. The types with small scissors and tweezers are best

Cordage - Any medium weight nylon cord will work. If you need to make a shelter, you will want as much cordage as you can find.

Cash & Documents. Have some extra cash, plus a copy of all your important documents (SS Card, I.D., fishing and hunting license, gun license). Pictures help to identify missing family.

Firearm(s) and Ammunition – A water pistol, filled with ammonia, works well to keep predators away. Weapons cause more problems than they solve.

Water – A quart per day (per person), as water is very heavy and portable filters are very light. Only carry water if you are in an area where it is scarce. This should include filters, and a metal canteen cup, and water purifying tablets.

Multi-Vitamins - Your nutrition will likely be poor, and you do not want to risk getting sick, vitamins and supplements become important.

Extra Medicine - As needed, because of pre-existing conditions.

Navigation – Should include a compass, maps, and GPS. Take the time to learn how to navigate with a compass.

Fishing Gear – Bobbers, hooks, fishing line, small a collapsible pole

Emergency Food - Food that will last and give you the most bang for your buck (peanut butter, jerky, sardines, granola bars, salt, and dried fruit).

Shelter - Sleeping bag, tent, tarp, and a light-weight thermal blanket

Extra Batteries and/or solar charging system.

Signal Devices - Flares, signaling mirror, and a whistle (on a string). Each person should have a whistle, prior to leaving the house.

Duct Tape - It can be used for everything, from making a splint to patching a container.

Other - Candles, safety pins, sewing needles and thread, entertainment (playing cards), wire for snaring.

This may seem like a lot of items, but if this becomes your total available supplies, you will be grateful for every item. If possible, go out camping and get more of a sense what it may be like if you only had what you could carry.

Remember Katrina, when many people had to leave their homes on such very short notice? To this day some of them have never been able to return. You may only get one chance, and that's it. With a bit of preparation, you can make it count.

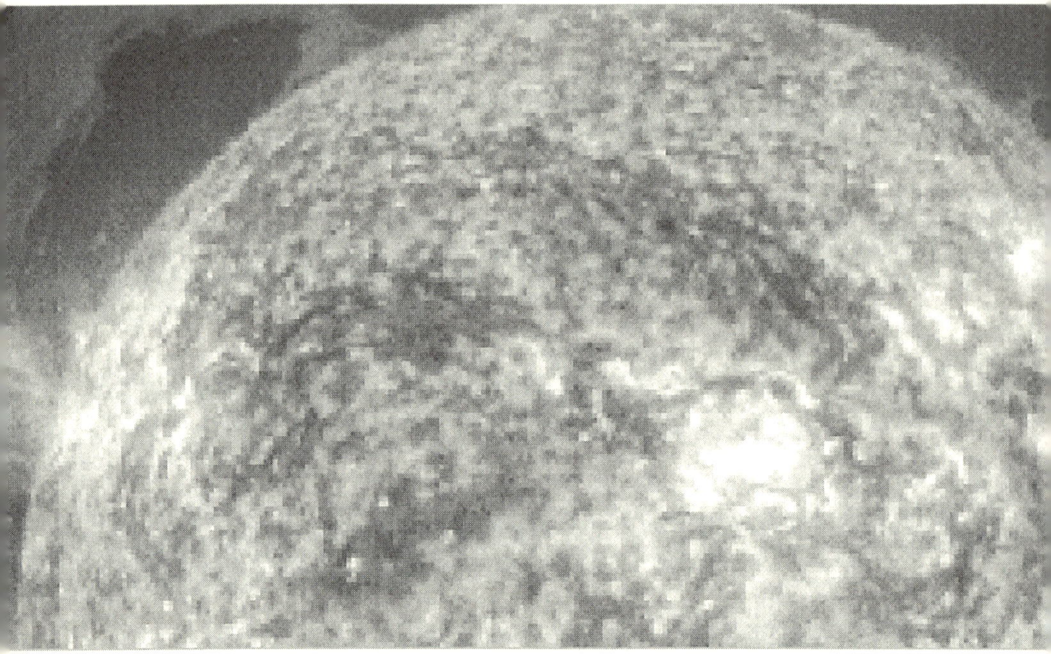

Coronal Mass Ejection (CME), SOHO image, June 9, 2002

400 Chernobyls - Solar Flares, Grid Collapse and Nuclear Armageddon

by Matthew Stein, P.E.

[*Nexus Magazine*, February-March, 2012, page 12-26]

There are nearly 450 nuclear reactors in the world, with hundreds more either under construction or in the planning stages. There are 104 of these reactors in the USA and 195 in Europe. Imagine what havoc it would wreak on our civilization and the planet's ecosystems if we were to suddenly witness not just one or two nuclear melt-downs but 400 or more! How likely is it that our world might experience an event that could ultimately cause hundreds of reactors to fail and melt down at approximately the same time? I venture to say that, unless we take significant protective measures, this apocalyptic scenario is not only possible but probable.

Consider the ongoing problems caused by three reactor core meltdowns, explosions, and breached containment vessels at Japan's Fukushima Daiichi facility, and the subsequent health and environmental issues. Consider the millions of innocent victims that have already died or continue to suffer from horrific radiation-related health problems ("Chernobyl AIDS", epidemic cancers, chronic fatigue, etc) resulting from the Chernobyl reactor explosions,

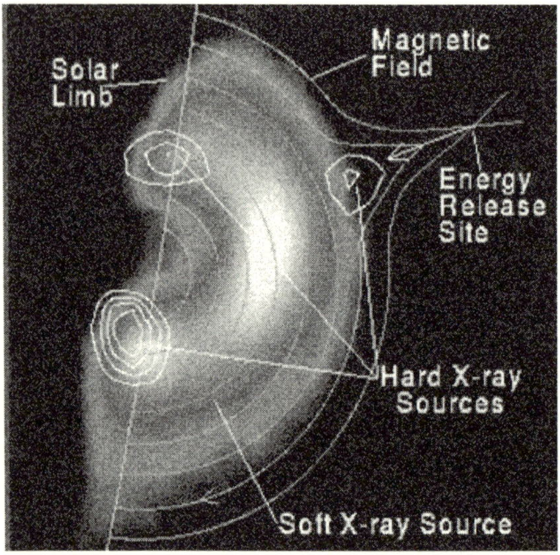

fires, and fallout. If just two serious nuclear disasters, spaced 25 years apart, could cause such horrendous environmental catastrophes, it is hard to imagine how we could ever hope to recover from hundreds of similar nuclear incidents occurring simultaneously across the planet. Since more than one third of all Americans live within 50 miles of a nuclear power plant, this is a serious issue that should be given top priority![1]

Since an extreme GMD of such a potentially disruptive magnitude that it would collapse the grid across most of the US last occurred in May of 1921, long before the advent of modern electronics, widespread electric power grids, and nuclear power plants, we are for the most part blissfully unaware of this threat and totally unprepared for its consequences. The good news is that relatively affordable equipment and processes could be installed to protect critical components in the electric power grid and its nuclear reactors, thereby averting this "end-of-the-world-as-we-know-it" scenario. The bad news is that even though panels of scientists and engineers have studied the problem, and the bi-partisan congressional EMP commission has presented a list of specific recommendations to congress, our leaders have yet to approve and implement a single significant preventative measure!

Most of us believe something like this could never happen, and if it could, certainly our "authorities" would do everything in their power to make sure they would prevent such an Apocalypse from ever taking place. Unfortunately, the opposite is true. "How could this happen?" you might ask. "Is this truly possible?" Read and weep, for you will soon know the answer.

Nuclear Power Plants and the Electric Power Grid

Our global system of electrical power generation and distribution ("the grid"), upon which every facet of our modern life is utterly dependent, in its current form is extremely vulnerable to severe geomagnetic storms of a magnitude that tends to strike our planet on an average of approximately once every 70 to 100 years. We depend on this grid to maintain food production and distribution, telecommunications, Internet services, medical services, military defense, transportation, government, water treatment, sewage and garbage removal, refrigeration, oil refining and gas pumping, and to conduct all forms of commerce.

Unfortunately, the world's nuclear power plants, as they are currently designed, are critically dependent upon maintaining connection to a functioning electrical grid, for all but relatively short periods of electrical blackouts, in order to keep their reactor cores continuously cooled so as to avoid catastrophic reactor core meltdowns and spent fuel rod storage pond fires.

If an extreme GMD were to cause widespread grid collapse (which it most certainly will), in as little as one or two hours after each nuclear reactor facility's backup generators either fail to start, or run out of fuel, the reactor cores will start to melt down. After a few days without electricity to run the cooling system pumps, the water bath covering the spent fuel rods stored in "spent fuel ponds" will boil away, allowing the stored fuel rods to melt down and burn [2]. Since the Nuclear Regulatory Commission (NRC) currently mandates that only one week's supply of backup generator fuel needs to be stored at each reactor site, it is likely that after we witness the spectacular night-time celestial light show from the next extreme GMD we will have about one week in which to prepare ourselves for Armageddon.

To do nothing is to behave like ostriches with our heads in the sand, blindly believing that "everything will be okay," as our world inexorably drifts towards the next naturally recurring, 100% inevitable, super solar storm and resultant extreme GMD. The result of which in short order will end the industrialized world as we know it, incurring almost incalculable suffering, death, and environmental destruction on a scale not seen since the extinction of the dinosaurs some 65 million years ago.

The End of "The Grid" As We Know It

There are records from the 1850s to today of roughly one hundred significant geomagnetic solar storms, two of which in the last 25 years were strong enough to cause millions of dollars worth of damage to key components that keep our modern grid powered. In March of 1989, a severe solar storm induced powerful electric currents in grid wiring that fried a main power transformer in the HydroQuebec system, causing a cascading grid failure that knocked out power to 6 million customers for nine hours while also damaging similar transformers in New Jersey and the United Kingdom. More recently, in 2003 a solar storm of lesser intensity, but longer duration, caused a blackout in Sweden and induced powerful currents in the South African grid that severely damaged or destroyed fourteen of their major power transformers, impairing commerce and comfort over major portions of that country as they were forced to resort to massive rolling blackouts that dragged on for many months[3].

During the Great Geomagnetic Storm of May 14-15, 1921, brilliant aurora displays were reported in the Northern Hemisphere as far south as Mexico and Puerto Rico, and in the Southern Hemisphere as far north as Samoa[5].

Transformer at the Salem Nuclear Plant,
damaged by March 1989 solar storm[4].

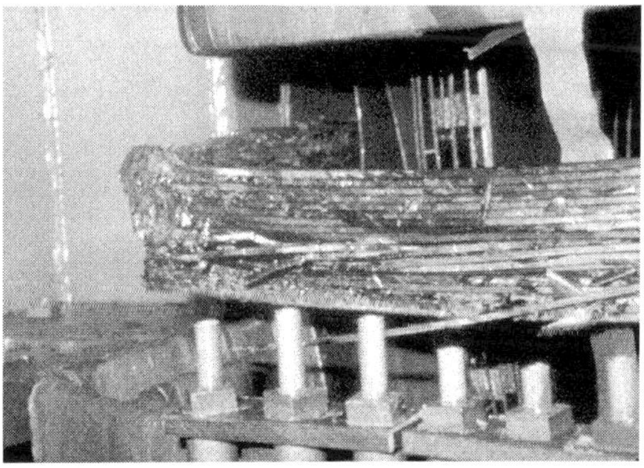

This extreme GMD produced ground currents roughly ten times as strong as the 1989 Quebec incident. Just 62 years earlier, the great granddaddy of recorded GMDs, referred to as "The Carrington Event," raged from August 28 to September 4, 1859. This extreme GMD induced currents so powerful that telegraph lines, towers, and stations caught on fire at a number of locations around the world. Best estimates are that the Carrington Event was approximately 50% stronger than the Great Geomagnetic Storm of 1921[6]. Since we are headed into an active solar period, much like the one preceding the Carrington Event, scientists are concerned that conditions could be ripe for the next extreme GMD[7].

Prior to the advent of the microchip and modern extra-high-voltage (EHV) transformers (key grid components that were first introduced in the late 1960's), most electrical systems were relatively robust and resistant to the effects of GMDs. Given the fact that a simple electrostatic spark can fry a microchip, and many thousands of miles of power lines act like giant antennas for capturing massive amounts of GMD spawned electromagnetic energy, the electrical systems of the modern world are far more vulnerable than their predecessors.

The federal government recently sponsored a detailed scientific study to more fully understand the extent to which critical components of our national electrical power grid might be effected by either a naturally occurring GMD or a man-made EMP. Under the auspices of the EMP Commission and the Federal Emergency Management Agency (FEMA), and reviewed in depth by the Oakridge National Laboratory and the National Academy of Sciences, Metatech Corporation undertook extensive modeling and analysis of the potential effects of extreme geomagnetic storms upon the U.S. electrical power grid. Based upon a storm of intensity equal to the Great Geomagnetic Storm of 1921, Metatech estimated that within the US induced voltage and current spikes, combined with harmonic anomalies, would severely damage or destroy over 350 EHV power transformers critical to the functioning of the U.S. grid, and possibly well over 2000 EHV transformers worldwide.[4]

Growth of the US High Voltage Transmission Network
and the Annual Electric Energy [4]

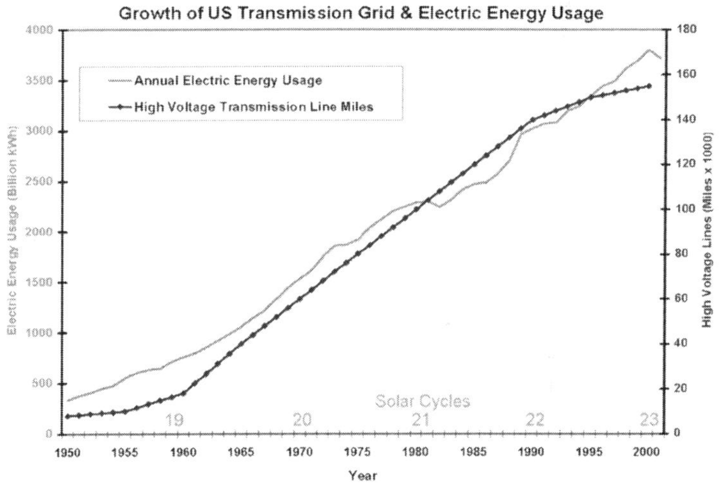

EHV transformers are custom designed for each installation and are made to order, weighing as much as 300 tons each, and costing well over US 1$ million each. Given the fact that there is currently a three year waiting list for a single EHV transformer (due to recent demand from China and India, the lead times have grown from one to three years), and that the total global manufacturing capacity is roughly 100 EHV transformers per year when the world's manufacturing centers are functioning properly, you can begin to grasp the dire implications of this situation.

The loss of thousands of EHV transformers worldwide would cause a catastrophic collapse of the grid, stretching across much of the industrialized world. It will take years at best for the industrialized world to put itself back together after such an event, especially considering the fact that most of the manufacturing centers that make this equipment will also be grappling with widespread grid failure.

Our Nuclear "Achilles Heel"

Five years ago I visited the still highly contaminated areas of Ukraine and the Belarus border where much of the radioactive plume from Chernobyl descended on 26 April 1986. I challenge chief scientist John Beddington and environmentalists like George Monbiot or any of the pundits now downplaying the risks of radiation to talk to the doctors, the scientists, the mothers, children and villagers who have been left with the consequences of a major nuclear accident. It was grim. We went from hospital to hospital and from one contaminated village to another. We found deformed and genetically mutated babies in the wards; pitifully sick children in the homes; adolescents with stunted growth and dwarf torsos; fetuses without thighs or fingers and villagers who told us every member of their family was sick. This was 20 years after the accident, but we heard of many unusual clusters of people with rare bone cancers.... Villages testified that 'the Chernobyl necklace' —thyroid cancer—was so common as to be unremarkable.

— John Vidal, "Nuclear's Green Cheerleaders Forget Chernobyl at Our Peril," *Guardian. co.uk*, April 1, 2011[8]

So what do extended grid blackouts have to do with potential nuclear catastrophes? Nuclear power plants are designed to disconnect automatically from the grid in the event of a local power failure or major grid anomaly, and once disconnected they begin the process of shutting down the reactor's core. In the event of the loss of coolant flow to an active nuclear reactor's core, the reactor will start to melt down and fail catastrophically within a matter of a few hours at most. In an extreme GMD, nearly every reactor in the world could be affected.

It was a short-term cooling system failure that caused the partial reactor core melt-down in March 1979 at Three Mile Island, Pennsylvania. Similarly, according to Japanese authorities it was not direct damage from Japan's 9.0 magnitude Tohoku Earthquake on March 11, 2011 that caused the Fukushima Daiichi nuclear reactor disaster, but the loss of electric power to the reactor's cooling system pumps when the reactor's backup batteries and diesel generators were wiped out by the ensuing tidal waves. In the hours and days after the tidal waves shuttered the cooling systems, the cores of reactors number 1, 2, and 3 were in full meltdown and released hydrogen gas, fueling explosions which breached several reactor containment vessels and blew the roof off the building housing the spent fuel storage pond of reactor number 4.

Of even greater danger and concern than the reactor cores themselves are the spent fuel rods stored in on-site cooling ponds. Lacking a permanent spent nuclear fuel storage facility, so-called "temporary" nuclear fuel containment ponds are features common to nearly all nuclear reactor facilities. They typically contain the accumulated spent fuel from 10 or more decommissioned reactor cores. Due to lack of a permanent repository, most of these fuel containment ponds are greatly overloaded and tightly packed beyond original design. They are generally surrounded by common light industrial buildings, with concrete walls and corrugated steel roofs. Unlike the active reactor cores, which are encased inside massive "containment vessels" with thick walls of concrete and steel, the buildings surrounding spent fuel rod storage ponds would do practically nothing to contain radioactive contaminants in the event of prolonged cooling system failures.

Since spent fuel ponds typically hold far greater quantities of highly radioactive material then the active nuclear reactors locked inside reinforced containment vessels, they clearly present far greater potential for the catastrophic spread of highly radioactive contaminants over huge swaths of land, polluting the environment for multiple generations spanning hundreds of years. A study by the Nuclear Regulatory Commission (NRC) determined that the "boil down time" for spent fuel rod containment ponds runs from between 4 and 22 days after loss of cooling system power before degenerating into a Fukushima-like situation, depending upon the type of nuclear reactor and how recently its latest batch of fuel rods had been decommissioned[9].

Reactor fuel rods have a protective zirconium cladding, which if superheated while exposed to air will burn with intense self-generating heat, much like a magnesium fire, releasing highly radioactive aerosols and smoke. According to Arnie Gundersen, former Senior Vice President for Nuclear Engineering Services Corporation, now turned nuclear whistle-blower, once a zirconium fire has started, due to its extreme temperatures and high degree of reactivity, contact with water will result in the water dissociating into hydrogen and oxygen gases, which will almost certainly lead to violent explosions. Gundersen says that once a zirconium fuel rod fire has started, the worst thing you could do is to try to quench the fire with water streams, since this action will only make matters worse and lead to violent explosions. Gundersen believes the massive explosion that blew the roof off the spent fuel pond at Fukushima was caused by zirconium induced hydrogen dissociation[10].

Had it not been for heroic efforts on the part of Japan's nuclear workers to replenish waters in the spent fuel pool at Fukushima, those spent fuel rods

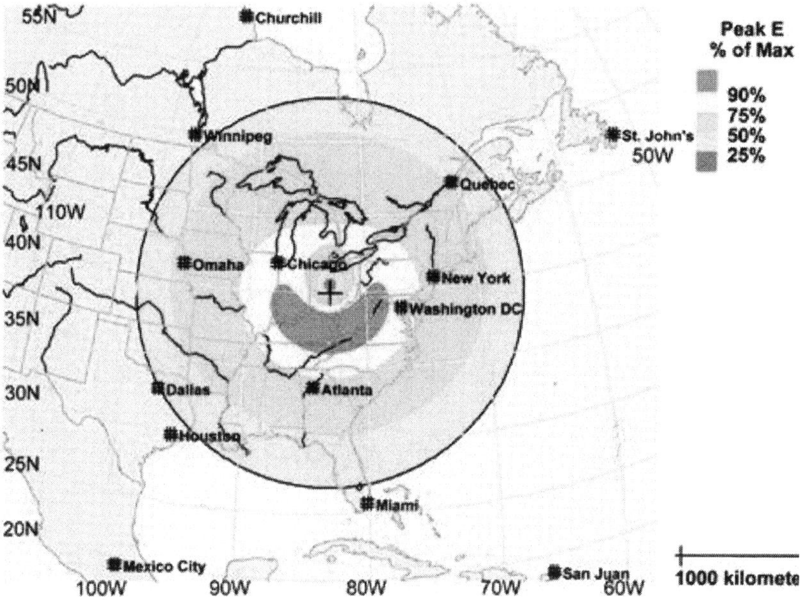

Illustrative EMP effects—Fast Pulse E1 Effects. [11]

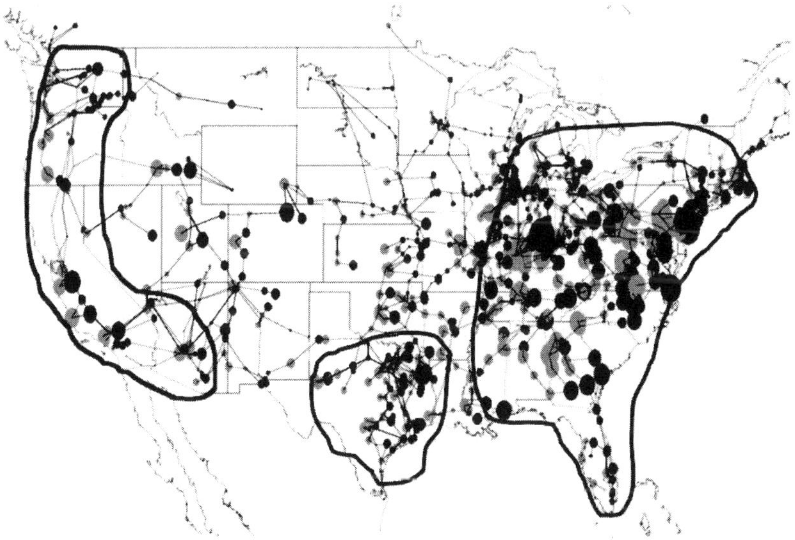

Severe geomagnetic storm with a 45 degree geomagnetic disturbance scenario. The above regions outlined are susceptible to system collapse due to the effects of extreme GMD disturbance. [10]

would have melted down and ignited their zirconium cladding, which most likely would have released far more radioactive contamination than what came from the three reactor core melt-downs. Japanese officials have estimate that the Fukushima Daiichi nuclear disaster has already released into the local environment just over half the total radioactive contamination as was released by Chernobyl, but other sources estimate it could be significantly more than was released by the accident at Chernobyl. In the event that an extreme GMD induced long-term grid collapse covering much of the globe, if just half of the world's spent fuel ponds were to boil off their water and become radioactive zirconium fed infernos, the ensuing contamination could far exceed the cumulative effect of 400 *Chernobyls.*

Electromagnetic Pulse (EMP) Attack

> Many of the control systems we considered achieved optimal connectivity through Ethernet cabling. EMP coupling of electrical transients to the cables proved to be an important vulnerability during threat illumination.... The testing and analysis indicate that the electronics could be expected to see roughly 100 to 700 ampere current transients on typical Ethernet cables. Effects noted in EMP testing occurred at the lower end of this scale. The bottom line observation at the end of the testing was that every system failed when exposed to the simulated EMP environment.
>
> — Report of the Commission to Asses the Threat to the United States from Electromagnetic Pulse (EMP) Attack[11]

Electromagnetic pulses (EMPs) and solar super storms are two different, but related, categories of events that are often described as high-impact, low frequency (HILF) events. Events categorized as HILF don't happen very often, but if and when they do they have the potential to severely affect the lives of many millions of people. Think of an EMP as a super-powerful radio wave capable of inducing damaging voltage spikes in electrical wires and electronic devices across vast geographical areas. (Note that the geomagnetic effects of solar storms are also described as "natural EMP".)

What is generally referred to as an EMP strike is the deliberate detonation of a nuclear device at a high altitude, roughly defined as somewhere between 24 and 240 miles (40 and 400 kilometers) above the surface of the earth. Nuclear detonations of this type have the potential to cause serious damage to electronics and electrical power grids along their line of sight, covering huge distances on the order of a circular area 1,500 miles (2,500 kilometers) in diameter, which would correspond to an area stretching roughly from Quebec City in Canada down to Dallas, Texas.

The concern is that some rogue state or terrorist organization might build their own nuclear device from scratch or buy one illegally, procure a Scud missile (or similar) on the black market and launch their nuclear device from a large fishing boat or freighter somewhere off the coast of the US, causing grid collapse and widespread damage to electronic devices across roughly 50% of America. Much like an extreme GMD, a powerful EMP attack would also cause widespread grid collapse, but it would be limited to a much smaller geographical area.

A powerful EMP from a sub-orbital nuclear detonation would cause extreme electromagnetic effects, starting with an initial short duration "speed of light" pulse, referred to as an "E1" effect, followed by a middle duration pulse called an "E2" effect, which is followed by a longer duration disturbance known as an "E3" effect. The "E1" effect lasts on the order of a few nanoseconds, and is quite similar to massive discharges of electrostatic sparks, which are particularly damaging to digital microelectronic chips that are at the core of most modern electronic equipment.

The intermediate "E2" effects last a fraction of a second, and are similar to many thousands to millions of lightning strikes hitting over a widespread area at almost exactly the same time. In the case of a nuclear induced EMP, its E3 effect starts after about a half second and may continue for several minutes. The E3 effect can be thought of as a "long slow burn", and electromagnetically it is quite similar to the effects from an extreme GMD, except that the latter may continue for a number of hours or days.

A "successful" EMP attack launched against the US would most likely result in the immediate collapse of the grid across roughly 50% of the country, crash the stock market, and cause critical failures in many of the electronic systems in affected areas that control nuclear reactors, chemical plants, telecommunications systems and industrial processes. These systems include programmable logic controllers (PLC), digital control systems (DCS), and supervisory control and data acquisition systems (SCADA).

The only good news about EMP strike is that its effect will cover a much smaller area than an extreme GMD, so there will be a significant portion of the rest of the US, as well as the rest of the outside world, left intact and able to lend a hand towards rebuilding critical infrastructure in the affected areas. Imagine the near total loss of a functioning infrastructure across an area of about a million square miles (approximately 1.6 million square kilometers, roughly equivalent to 50 Hurricane Katrinas happening simultaneously) and you will have some idea of the potentially crippling effect of an EMP attack from a single medium sized sub-orbital nuclear detonation!

Preventing Armageddon

The congressionally mandated EMP Commission has studied the threat of both EMP and extreme GMD events, and made recommendations to the US congress to implement protective devices and procedures to insure the survival of the grid and other critical infrastructures in either event. John Kappenman, author of the Metatech study, estimates that it would cost on the order of $1 billion to build special protective devices into the US grid to protect its EHV transformers from EMP or extreme GMD damage, and to build stores of critical replacement parts should some of these items be damaged or destroyed. Kappenman estimates that it would cost significantly less than $1 billion to store at least a year's worth of diesel fuel for backup generators at each US nuclear facility and to store sets of critical spare parts, such as backup generators, inside EMP-hardened steel containers to be available for quick change-out in the event that any of these items were damaged by an EMP or GMD[12].

For the cost of a single B-2 bomber or a tiny fraction of the *TARP* bank bailout, we could invest in preventative measures to avert what might well become the end of our civilization and life as we know it! There is no way to protect against all possible effects from an extreme GMD or an EMP attack, but certainly we could implement measures to protect against the worst effects. Since 2008, Congress has narrowly failed to pass legislation that would implement at least some of the EMP Commission's recommendations[13].

We have a long ways to go to make our world EMP and GMD safe. Every citizen can do their part to push for legislation to move towards this goal, and to work inside our homes and communities to develop local resilience and self reliance, so that in the event of a long term grid-down scenario, we might make the most of a bad situation. The same tools that are espoused by the "Transition Movement" for developing local self-reliance and resilience to help cope with the twin effects of climate change and peak oil could also serve communities well in the event of an EMP attack or extreme GMD. If our country were to implement safeguards to protect our grid and nuclear power plants from EMP, it would also eliminate the primary incentive for a terrorist to launch an EMP attack. The sooner we take these actions the less chance that an EMP attack will occur!

For more information, or to get involved, see http://empactamerica.org/, http://survive-emp.com/, and http://www.transitionnetwork.org/ or contact your congressman at http://www.contactingthecongress.org/.

NOTES:

[1] Bill Dedman, "Nuclear Neighbors: Population Rises Near Nuclear Reactors," *MSNBC.com*. Available at http://www.msnbc.msn.com/id/42555888/ns/us_news-life/t/nuclear-neighbors-population-rises-near-us-reactors/#. Accessed December 2011.

[2] Dina Cappiello, "Long Blackouts Pose Risk to U.S. Nuclear Reactors," *Associated Press*, March 29, 2011.

[3] Lawrence E. Joseph, "The Sun Also Surprises," *New York Times*, August 15, 2010. Available at http://www.nytimes.com/2010/08/16/opinion/16joseph.html. Accessed August 2010.

[4] John Kappenman, "Geomagnetic Storms and Their Impacts on the U.S. Power Grid," *Metatech Corporation*, prepared for *Oak Ridge National Laboratory*, Meta-R-319, January 2010, p. 2—29.

[5] S. M. Silverman and E. W. Cliver, "Low-Altitude Auroras: The Magnetic Storm of 14-15 May 1921," Journal of Atmospheric and Solar-Terrestrial Physics 63, (2001), p. 523-535. Additionally, "High-Impact, Low-Frequency Event Risk to the North American Bulk Power System: A Jointly Commissioned Summary Report of the North American Electric Reliability Corporation and the U.S. Department of Energy's November 2009 Workshop," June, 2010, p. 68.

[6] Committee on the Societal and Economic Impacts of Severe Space Weather Events: A Workshop National Research Council, "Severe Space Weather

Events: Understanding Societal and Economic Impacts Workshop Report," National Research Council of the National Academies (2008), p. 7-13, and p. 100. Additionally, E. W. Cliver and L. Svalgaard, "The 1859 Solar-Terrestrial Disturbance and the Current Limits of Extreme Space Weather Activity," *Solar Physics* (2004) 224, P. 407-422.

[7] Richard A. Lovett, "What if the Biggest Solar Storm on Record Happened Today?" *National Geographic News*, March 2, 2011. Available at

http://news.nationalgeographic.com/news/2011/03/110302-solar-flares-sun-storms-earth-danger-carrington-event-science/.

[8] John Vidal, "Nuclear's Green Cheerleaders Forget Chernobyl at Our Peril," *Guardian.co.uk*, April 1, 2011. Available at

http://www.guardian.co.uk/commentisfree/2011/apr/01/fukushima-chernobyl-risks-radiation. Accessed May 2011.

[9] NUREG-1738, "Technical Study of Spent Fuel Pool Accident Risk at Decommissioning Nuclear Power Plants," February 2001, as reported in "Petition for Rulemaking: Docket No. PRM-50-96," Foundation for Resilient Societies before the Nuclear Regulatory Commission, p. 3-9 and 49-50. Available at

http://www.resilientsocieties.org/images/Petition_For_Rulemaking_Resilient_Societies_Docketed.pdf

[10] Arnold Gundersen, interview by author, November 2011.

[11] "Report of the Commission to Assess the Threat to the United States from Electromagnetic Pulse (EMP) Attack: Critical National Infrastructures," April, 2008, p. 6.

[12] John Kappenman, interview by author, December 2011.

[13] Dr. Peter Vincent Pry, "Statement Before the Congressional Caucus on EMP," *EMPact America*, February 15, 2011. Available at http://www.empacta-merica.org/pry-statement-to-emp-caucus.pdf. Accessed November 2011.

About the Author

Matthew Stein is a design engineer, green builder, and author of two best-selling books: *When Disaster Strikes: A Comprehensive Guide to Emergency Planning and Crisis Survival* (Chelsea Green 2011), and *When Technology Fails: A Manual for Self-Reliance, Sustainability, and Surviving the Long Emergency* (Chelsea Green 2008).

Stein is a graduate of the Massachusetts Institute of Technology (MIT) where he majored in Mechanical Engineering. Stein has appeared on numerous radio and television programs and is a repeat guest on F*ox News, Lionel, Coast-to-Coast AM*, and the *Thom Hartmann Show.* He is an active mountain climber, serves as a guide and instructor for blind skiers, has written several articles on the subject of sustainable living, and is a guest columnist for the *Huffington Post.*

Current titles by Dr. Richard Alan Miller

Power Tools for the 21st Century
Toward the Evolution of Consciousness
$21.00
6x9"; delux color soft cover; black and white interior; 250 pages; contains explanitory illustrations and historic photos from the author's past during the time of his Navy SEAL curriculum development.
ISBN 978-0-9883379-2-3
Author: Dr. Richard Alan Miller

These are the protocols that were developed for the Navy SEALs to create super soldiers. these Power Tools can be used today for your own personal evolution of consciousness.

"Dr. Richard Alan Miller is one of the pioneers in the study of the paranormal. From studies designed to enhance military performance, he has created invaluable tools for living life in the 21st century. These techniques and processes can help you develop your own conscious evolution, and help you find your purpose in life."

Stanley Krippner, Ph.D., co-author, *Extraordinary Dreams and How to Use Them*

Workbook 1
Exercise Supplement for Power Tools for the 21st Century

$12.00
6x9"; delux color soft cover; black and white interior; 68 pages; contains explanitory illustrations and historic photos from the author's past during the time of his Navy SEAL curriculum development.
ISBN 978-0-9883379-3-0
Author: Dr. Richard Alan Miller

An exercise supplement for the 2nd book in the series Toward the Evolution of Consciousness this book features eight main training focuses. It includes self testing exercises, systems of cosmology and philosophy at the heart of developing one's consciousness and clearly defined meditation practices to achieve your goals.

These are the protocols that were developed for the Navy SEALs to create super soldiers. these Power Tools can be used today for your own personal evolution of consciousness.

ESP Induction
Through Forms of Self-Hypnosis

$18.00
6x9"; delux color soft cover; black and white interior; 214 pages; illustrated.
ISBN 978-1-890693-30-5
Author: Dr. Richard Alan Miller

The first book in the three book series written by Dr. Richard Alan Miller — Toward the Evolution of Consciousness, and an how-to book intended to increase a person's intuition and extra sensory perception (ESP) or sixth sense. The protocols identified here have been tested and found reliable in increasing a person's intuition or guessing ability by up to 400% above an individual's beginning levels. The book introduces basic information on self-hypnosis as a tool fir enhancing our latent human potentils or, as they are referred to in some military literature these days our anomalous human potentials peviously called ESP.

These are the protocols that were developed for the Navy SEALs to create super soldiers. these Power Tools can be used today for your own personal evolution of consciousness.

Native Plants of Commercial Importance
The Nomadic Life of the Professional Forager
A book for the Wildcrafter and Herb Farmer

$20.00
6x9"; delux color soft cover; black and white interior; 344 pages; fully illustrated.
ISBN 978-0-9883379-0-9
Author: Dr. Richard Alan Miller

Here is an information-filled look at how to supplement rural incomes by the harvest of native plants from the region. Among the wild plants of North America are many which have long been used in medicinal, cosmetic, food and floral industries. Some of them are used in sufficient quantities to make them commercially important.

The book describes these and other forest products, dividing North America into five regions: Northeast, South, Midwest, Southwest and the Northwest. Each region contains a descriptions of 10 common crops now harvested, with detail and a special appendix on marketing. Reforestation is stressed to make each crop renewable and self-generating as a natural resource. This technique has led to the new concept of Forest Farming.

The future of foraging as a source of supplementing one's rural income lies with our ability to recognize natural resources.

The Encyclopedia for Alternative Agriculture
For Urban and Semi-Rural Communities

$24.95
Large format, 8.5x11"; delux color soft cover; black and white interior; 216 pages.
ISBN 978-0-9883379-1-6
Author: Dr. Richard Alan Miller

The Encyclopedia of Alternative Agriculture: For the Urban and Semi-Rural Communities is an anthology of approximately 120 newsletters over a 10 year period called, The Herb Market Report. Each issue features 2 herbs, one on small farm alternatives and the other on a forage crop. Each also includes a farm/forage plan, harvest and drying techniques, processing and storage requirements, and marketing options. A cottage industry section is featured as well. The articles are in depth, concerning all aspects of herb production, processing and marketing for active and potential herb farmers.They teach the basics for how to "small farm" field crops correctly, and be successful. Book 1 contains the first 24 newsletters.

The author, Dr. Richard Alan Miller, is a world renowned agricultural consultant and researcher on the forefront and 'cutting edge' of the sciences related to botanicals and their practical cultivation, use and marketing.

THE MODERN ALCHEMIST
A Guide to Personal Transformation
RICHARD AND IONA MILLER
With Illustrations by Joel Radcliffe

THE MAGICAL AND RITUAL USE OF
HERBS
Richard Alan Miller

THE MAGICAL AND RITUAL USE OF
PERFUMES
Richard Alan Miller and Iona Miller

THE MAGICAL AND RITUAL USE OF
APHRODISIACS

Current titles by Dr. Richard Alan Miller

For a full listing of publications for sale, the current schedule and blog reports please go to www.richardalanmiller.com and www.docram.com.

The Magical and Ritual Use of Herbs	$ 12.95
The Magical and Ritual Use of Aphrodisiacs	$ 12.95
The Magical and Ritual Use of Perfumes	$ 18.95
The Potential of Herbs as a Cash Crop	$ 20.00
Native Plants of Commercial Importance	$ 20.00
The Encyclopedia of Alternative Agriculture – Vol. 1/5	$ 24.95
Vol. 2/5	in press
Vol. 3/5	in press
Vol. 4/5	in press
Vol. 5/5	in press
ESP Induction through forms of Self-Hypnosis	$ 18.00
Power Tools for the 21st Century	$ 21.00
Workbook 1	$ 12
Workbook 2	$ 12
Workbook 3	in press
The Non-Local Min in a Holographic Universe	in press
The Modern Alchemist	$ 20.00
Pantheon: Archetypal God in Daily Living	in press

OAK

OAK Publishing

Organization for Advancement of Knowledge

Grants Pass, Oregon 97527 USA

Dr. Richard Alan Miller is a pioneer in the annals of metaphysical and paranormal exploration. Miller began working in the "X-Files" world of Navy Intel (Seal Corp. and then MRU) in the late 60's. His public collaborations and research continue.

As an original black ops team-member, Miller's research in the field of paranormal began as a graduate physicist working 11 years with Navy Intel (Anesthesiology). During this period numerous foundational papers, including "*A Holographic Concept of Reality*" and "*Embryonic Holography*" were written.

His past and current writings and presentations reveal a depth of knowledge and practical experience in three major fields; Alternative Agriculture, New Age Physics, and Metaphysics.

Miller now writes for Nexus magazine and is a preferred guest on internet radio. He is re-emerging at a critical time in humanities evolution where metaphysics and practical survival converge.

For a full listing of publications for sale, the current schedule and blog reports please go to www.richardalanmiller.com and www.docram.com.